REALITY OF THE
SPIRITUAL WORLD

By THOMAS R. KELLY

PENDLE HILL PAMPHLET NUMBER TWENTY-ONE

Printing Statement:

Due to the very old age and scarcity of this book, many of the pages may be hard to read due to the blurring of the original text, possible missing pages, missing text and other issues beyond our control.

Because this is such an important and rare work, we believe it is best to reproduce this book regardless of its original condition.

Thank you for your understanding.

FOREWORD

Throughout his years at Haverford College Thomas R. Kelly entered generously into the life of Pendle Hill. To Haverford–Pendle Hill students he gave both instruction and inspiration. He was lecturer in the summer term of 1936, and he visited us at many other times as a member of the American Friends Service Committee and of various other groups conferring here. He was always a warm friend óf Pendle Hill and its purposes.

The second Sunday in January, 1941, he spent at Pendle Hill, leading a conference of the Meeting workers on cultivation of the spiritual life. On many who heard him that day, at the height of his power and effectiveness, he made an unforgettable impression which was intensified by the news of his sudden death five days later.

For these and for reasons of personal friendship, it seems fitting that some word of his be included in the Pendle Hill pamphlet series. It is with gratitude that the Publication Committee has received from Lael Kelly the present series of four addresses, given during the winter of 1940–41, which is here published as Pamphlet Twenty-One.

Thomas R. Kelly's manuscript has been altered only in such verbal details as make it more suitable for print than for the spoken word.

Some of the material is similar to that in other of his writings; some is different, while some offers a fresh interpretation of the same truths.

Taken as a whole, these essays are a refreshing demonstration of the careful scholarship, the warm humanity, and the valid mystical experience which made so many of those who loved Thomas Kelly as a friend hearken to him as a prophet.

3

REALITY OF THE SPIRITUAL WORLD

GOD

How can we be sure that God is real, and not just a creation of our wishes? We have disquieting desires for a God, for a real God. There come to us times of loneliness when we seem to have a premonition of a deep vastness in ourselves, when the universe about us, gigantic as it is in all its starry depths, seems cramped and narrow for our souls, and something makes us long for an abiding Home. We have times of fatigue, of confusion, of exhaustion, of utter discouragement, when we long for a serene and everlasting Bosom on which to lay our heads and be at peace. But how can we be sure that what we call God is not a product of our wishful thinking, a self-delusion we create, a giant shadow of our longings flung up against the sky and asserted to be real?

We have moments when we long, not for freedom and yet more freedom, but for self-surrender, self-dedication, self-abandonment in utter loyalty to an Overself. If I could find an Object worthy of my utmost allegiance, if I could find a Mark worthy to be the aim of the bow of my life, I should gladly pull the arrow back to its head and let all fly upon a single shot. I should be integrated, freed from internal conflicts, those confusions and tangles

5

within which make me ineffective, indecisive, wavering, half-hearted, unhappy. I should gladly be a slave of such a Being, and know that I am truly free when I am His utter slave. But I see men and women, my brothers and sisters in Germany and Italy and Russia, who joyfully commit their all to the State, to an earthly state, to a state which to them seems noble, glorious, and ideal. They seem to get integration and joy in enslavement similar to that which my religious friends get from commitment to an invisible, spiritual world. Maybe the values all lie on the subjective side, on the integration of self and the dedication of will to *any* object which is conceived as worthy. Maybe the object doesn't have to be real but just to be thought to be real with a vigorous, fanatical intensity. I know that false ideas and misplaced enthusiasms have had as real effects upon men and upon history as have well-grounded beliefs and ideals. Maybe the whole conviction of a Spiritual Reality shadowing over us all is such a hoax, a useful hoax as long as we believe it intensely, a hoax that stabilizes men and society and one that ought to be preserved and nourished and fostered for its useful social effect. Such is the almost universal argument in the mind of educated man.

But there is an inner integrity in us all which rejects all programs of As If. We cannot merely act *as if* there were a God, while we secretly

6

keep our fingers crossed. This inner integrity demands the *real;* we cannot long tolerate complex ways of kidding ourselves, nor forever whistle to keep our courage up. It is an old maxim, with a double meaning: "Let the truth be known, though the heavens fall." We are such creatures as demand to build upon the Truth. And if the Truth is that there are no heavens, but only earth, no real God, but only human cravings for a God, then we want to know *that,* and adjust our lonely lives to that awful fact.

First Argument: Analogy

Caught in this difficulty, that we long for a Real God, no, demand a Real God, yet can be sure of only our subjective longings, not of God's objective existence, we ask a devout friend, "Are you sure that God is real?" And he replies, "Yes, I am absolutely sure." We then continue, "But why are you so sure there is a Reality, an actually existent reality corresponding to your religious cravings?" He replies, "I find myself in a world which furnishes real objects to answer all my central cravings In me, subjectively, there is a craving for food. And I find, out there, in the world, that the Universe furnishes me real food. In me I find a profound craving for companionship. And out in the world there are real men and women who give their fellowship in answer to my crav-

7

ing. In me is an insistent craving for sex. And I find myself set in a universe that furnishes real beings of the opposite sex. I find in myself a craving for beauty, and out there I find beautiful objects that satisfy my soul. And when I find in myself a profound craving for God, for an absolute resting place for my soul's devotion, an Object for my last loyalty, I believe that here, too, there is an answering Object. The same structural situation — subjective craving, satisfying Object — is to be expected."

"But," we answer, "you are arguing from analogy. And analogies are notoriously treacherous. You argue that the fact of food-hunger, with its answering object of real food, gives you the right to say, 'From the fact of God-hunger I am sure there is a real Bread of Life.' But analogies break down. If analogies were always perfect, they would cease to be analogies and become identities. No, the time comes when similar situations part company, and are different. Perhaps the matter of God's real existence is just such a case. One can't be sure. *And I want to be sure.* At best your argument from analogy only indicates the possibility that there is an objectively real God, corresponding to my hunger for Him. Perhaps it even indicates *probability*. But I want deeper grounds than that."

Second Argument: Authority

Disappointed in this first argument for the reality of a Spiritual Being wherein we may cradle our life, we turn in a second direction and ask a devout Protestant: "Do you believe that God is utterly real?" He replies, "Yes," and you ask, "Why?" to which he answers, "The Bible tells me God is real, that in Him we live and move and have our being." "But why do you believe the Bible?" To this he replies, "Because the Scriptures are inspired." You reply, "Yes, I strongly agree with you. But I suspect you and I may mean different things. Why do you say Scripture is inspired? Is it because you find in it the record of men who were drinking from the same fountains of life that well up in you, so that you, too, could write inspired words that would feed other hungry souls?" "Oh, no, no," he might hastily reply, "I am no such great soul. God chose special men to write the Scriptures, and I'm not one of them." To this you may reply, "I disagree, and am bold enough to believe that the fountains of inspiration are not stopped. There is no one age of inspiration, no one special class of inspired. Either divine inspiration is renewed in every age and in all peoples, or it never flowed at all. Now tell me, why do you believe the Bible is inspired so that you can rely upon its testimony to the reality of God?" He answers, "The Bible is inspired because it is written, 'All Scripture is given of God.' " "But wait. Do you mean to prove the Bible by the Bible? That is the crudest circle in argument. By the same argument the Book of Mormon is inspired, for it says it is, and therefore you must believe all Mormon teachings." Then he retreats and says, "But the Bible is an ancient and revered authority, tested by time, canonized by Councils, and believed by multitudes." You answer, "So are the Buddhist scriptures, such as the *Dhammapada* and *The Lotus of the Wonderful Law*. Your argument only amounts to this,' 'Forty million Frenchmen can't be wrong.' You only argue, 'Forty million or forty billion Christians can't be wrong in trusting the Bible.' But if you ask forty million Asiatics you'll get a different answer. You'll have to surrender the authority of the Bible if it is based upon the circular argument, 'The Bible is authoritative because it says authoritatively that it is authoritative.' After which you can't retreat into the argument, 'The Bible is a good and reliable authority because masses of people believe in it,' imposing as that fact is. Mass agreement, even upon the existence of God, is not enough to prove that God exists. Maybe the whole of mankind is deluded on the matter. That's just my problem. And you don't settle it for me by appealing to the authority of a revered Book, if that authority is guaranteed only by mass acceptance."

The authoritarian evidence for the reality of God as given by many Protestants, who make the Book the supreme authority, reappears in different form if an average Roman Catholic is approached. His final defense of the authority of the Bible might be that Holy Church guaranteed the reliability of the Bible, and of the widespread conviction that there is a really existent God. For did not the Church Fathers and the Councils and the Bible agree in this matter, that there is a God in heaven, brooding over the world in love? But long ago Abelard startled the Roman Church by printing a little book with each page in two columns, in which, without comment, he set side by side contradictory statements of the Fathers of the Church. Evidently authorities disagree. And when authorities disagree, who shall be the authority to choose between authorities? Roman Catholics would reply, "The Pope is infallible when he officially makes a decision." But you ask, "Who guarantees the infallibility of the Pope?" Answer: "The Vatican Council in 1870 pronounced the Pope infallible." But are Church Councils infallible, so that they can infallibly guarantee the infallibility of the Pope? No, only the Pope is infallible. And there you are with authoritarian guarantees of the reality of God fallen to the ground.

Third Argument: Causation

I shall take time to state only one more effort to prove the objective reality of the spiritual world. For, honestly, all these arguments leave me cold. Even if they were sound — and none of them is watertight — they would only quiet my intellectual questionings. They would never motivate me to absolute dedication to Him for whom I yearn. But religious men are dedicated men, joyously enslaved men, bondservants of God and of his Christ, given in will to God. Arguments are devised subsequent to our deep conviction, not preceding our conviction. They bolster faith; they do not create it.

The third argument is this: Here is a world, amazingly complex, astonishingly interknit. Here are flowers, depending upon bees for pollination, and bees dependent upon flowers for food. Yonder are the starry heavens, adjusted, maintained, wheeling their way through staggering spaces in perfect rhythm and order. Whence comes it all, if not from God? And here am I, a complex being, of amazing detail of body and astounding reaches of mind. Yet my parents didn't *make* me; they are as incapable of being my true cause as I am incapable of being the true cause of my children. This whole spectacle is too vast, too well articulated to be caused by any single thing *in* the world. There must be a cause outside and beneath the whole, which I call God, who creates, maintains, and preserves the whole world order.

Such an argument seems imposing and appealing to us all. But it is not absolutely watertight. For notice, this is not a perfect world, as we all know only too well from observation and experience. There are imperfections and flaws in it, notes that jar as well as notes that blend. The argument rests upon only half the evidence, the good in the world, not the evil and dislocation. There are maladjustments as well as adjustments. We may marvel at the human eye. But the great physicist Helmholtz said that if an optical workman made for him an apparatus as imperfect and inefficient as a human eye, he would dismiss him. Here is the point: You can't argue from an imperfect effect, the world, to a perfect cause, God. An imperfect effect can only legitimately imply an imperfect cause, not a perfect one. If a World Cause made this world, He was not omniscient, but had a streak of stupidity in Him, to have allowed flaws to creep in. Or else, if He was omniscient, He was not omnipotent, for, knowing what would be a world without flaws, He couldn't produce it. Again, if He was omniscient and omnipotent, but still made an imperfect world, then he was not omni-benevolent but malicious, and delighted in torturing his creation by creating men with dreams of perfection, yet tantalizingly setting them in a world that grinds out the dreams of their hearts.

And David Hume, knowing all this, added the suggestion, maybe the world is the result of a superhuman but not divine creator who used trial and error and bungled many worlds before he succeeded in making this one. Look at a modern ocean liner, amazingly compact and interdependent, seeming to imply a master mind behind it. And then be introduced to the ship-builder, who may be a very mediocre person, just a man like ourselves. He merely inherited the experience of repeated ship-builders over the centuries, each of whom was no master mind but just found out a little detail and added it to the heritage. Maybe the World-Creator is stupid and bungling, but given sufficiently repeated trials and errors He may turn out a fairly decent world.

Other Arguments Indicated

I shall not complete the list nor state the ontological argument, which argues from the notion of a perfect being involving its existence. Nor shall I state the moral argument, which argues that moral experience requires a God for its final validation. Nor shall I state the argument from the agreement of the race, from the universality of religion among all tribes of men, for I have referred to it already in pointing out that mass agreement cannot back up any belief in an authority.

But there is a wholly different way of being sure that God is real. It is not an intellectual proof, a reasoned sequence of thoughts. It is the fact that men *experience* the presence of God. Into our lives come times when, all unexpectedly, He shadows over us, steals into the inner recesses of our souls, and lifts us up in a wonderful joy and peace. The curtains of heaven are raised and we find ourselves in heavenly peace in Christ Jesus. Sometimes these moments of visitation come to us in strange surroundings — on lonely country roads, in a class room, at the kitchen sink. Sometimes they come in the hour of worship, when we are gathered into one Holy Presence who stands in our midst and welds us together in breathless hush, and wraps us all in sweet comfortableness into His arms of love. In such times of direct experience of Presence, we know that God is utterly real. We need no argument. When we are gazing into the sun we need no argument, no proof that the sun is shining.

This evidence for the reality of God is the one the Quakers primarily appeal to. It is the evidence upon which the mystics of all times rest their testimony. Quakerism is essentially empirical; it relies upon direct and immediate experience. We keep insisting: It isn't enough to *believe in* the love of God, as a doctrine; you must *experience* the love of God. It isn't enough to believe that Christ was born in Bethlehem, you must experience a Bethlehem, a birth of Christ in your hearts. To be able to defend a creed intellectually isn't enough; you must experience as reality first of all what the creed asserts. And unless the experience is there, behind it, the mere belief is not enough.

We must therefore examine this evidence from experience of God with some care, to see if it is sound, for it is crucial.

First, let us notice that this experience which seems so clearly to be an experience of God energizes us enormously, in a way far different from arguments. Arguments that convince our intellect alone leave us merely with questions answered, but they do not bring us to our knees in humble, joyful submission into His hands of all that we are. They do not bring the unutterable joy that makes Paul and Silas sing hymns at midnight in prison. Even though moments of the experience of Presence may dawn upon us, and then fade, we are thereafter new men and women, plowed through to our depths, ready to run and not be weary, and to walk and not faint. We love God with a new and joyous love, wholly and completely. It is no commanded love, it is the joyful answer of our whole being to His revealed love. Our will becomes dedicated, our self-offering to God is vitalized by deep emotional reinforcement. Such experiences of God make men and women who are the dynamic, creative, untiring workers of a group, for they are energized at the base of their being by a Divine Energizing. I believe the real vitality of religion rests upon the fact that religious experience is universally taking place. It isn't creeds that keep churches going, it is the dynamic of God's life, given in sublime and intimate moments to men and women and boys and girls.

Second, let us notice that the experience seems to come from beyond us. It doesn't seem to be a little subjective patch in our consciousness. It carries a sense of objectivity in its very heart, as if it arose from beyond us and came in as a revelation of a reality out there. If I may use a philosophic term, it is realistic. Just as my experience of that wall out there doesn't seem to be a subjective state of my mind, but a disclosure of a real wall out there beyond me, so the experience of God has in its inner nature a testimony that an Object is being disclosed to us. We do not make it, we receive it. There is a passivity on our part, and an independence of our own intention to experience God that is universally testified to. God seems to be the active one, we the receptive ones. And in glad discovery we know that God is dynamically at work in the world, and at work in us, pressing in upon us, knocking at the door of our minds and doing things to us which arise in His own initiative.

Third, let us notice that, for the person who experiences these apparent invasions, there is set up a state of certainty about God which is utterly satisfying and convincing to himself. It is not the certainty that follows upon a sound argument. It is different, a kind of self-guaranteeing certainty. It cannot be transferred to anyone else, but it is a certainty which is enough to convince oneself completely. St. Augustine says that after such experiences he was certain of God, but *in a new way*. Intellectual convincement of the reality of God is utterly different from the felt reality of God. One may have been intellectually convinced of God's existence, but the experience of God brings a new kind of meaning to the reality of God. He is real with a vividness and an indubitableness that is powerfully overwhelming to the individual. That inner certainty cannot be conveyed to another; it may only be caught by a contagion, as others see our lives and gain some intimation of the very springs of our being.

Now that we have given recognition to the testimony of experience, let us become more critical and intellectual. From a critical, intellectual point of view I believe that the testimony of mystic experience is not absolutely logically free from flaws. Just as all logical proofs for God's existence can be questioned, so the experiential evidence is not intellectually watertight, and we may as well face it, and be aware of it, as intellects. Yet I do not find my faith in the reality of the experience of God shaken by the fact that I can find intellectual holes in the testimony, any more than I find my faith shaken by discovering that all logical proofs for God's existence are defective. Such defects do not prove that God does not exist. They only drive us back to the old, old truth: we walk by faith and not by sight. Let us then be bold enough to face and acknowledge such criticism of the testimony of religious experience.

First, mere internal pressure of certainty does not prove certainty. Intense inner assurance that something is so does not make it so. The insane hospitals are full of people who have intense internal certainties that they are Jesus Christ, or Napoleon, or an angel from heaven. Shall we reject the internal pressure of certainty of the insane and keep the internal certainties of the sane? Medieval monks were internally certain that Satan whispered in their ear. If we accept some internal certainties, we should accept all, or else find some way of distinguishing between internal certainties. Not all can be true, or the world is a madhouse of contradictory certainties. I am persuaded that my experience of the presence of God is real, utterly real, that it originates in the invading love of God. But I must admit that, intellectually, my feeling of convincement is no more real and intense and, on this basis, no more reliable than the convincement of many people with whom I wholly disagree.

Second, if we retreat from this ground of assurance, we take refuge in a second assurance that our experience of God is grounded in a real God. This second assurance comes from the fact that lives that have experienced God as vividly real are new lives, transformed lives, stabilized lives, integrated lives, souls newly sensitive to moral needs of men, newly dynamic in transforming city slums and eradicating war. By their fruits we know that they have been touched, not by vague fancies, by subjective, diaphanous visions, but by a real, living Power. The consequences of the experience are so real that they must have been released by a real cause, a real God, a real Spiritual Power energizing them.

This pragmatic test, this pointing to the *fruits* of religious experience, is the most frequent defense of its validity. Not only Rufus Jones but all other writers on the subject make use of it. And it is very convincing.

But there is a logical defect in this pragmatic test. Be patient with me while I turn logician for a moment. The argument runs:

> If God has really visited us, He has transformed our lives.
> Our lives are transformed.
> Therefore He has visited us.

There is a patent logical fallacy in this argument, which is named the Fallacy of Affirming the Consequent. A valid form would be that of

Affirming the Antecedent, and would go like this:

> If God has really visited us, He has transformed our lives.
> He has visited us.
> Therefore He has transformed our lives.

But this form is of no use to us, for the minor·premise, "He has really visited us," is just the question, and cannot appear as a premise, but should appear in the conclusion. The only valid form in which "He has really visited us" can appear in the conclusion is in the negative form:

> If God has really visited us, He has transformed our lives.
> Our lives are not transformed.
> Therefore He has not really visited us.

But this valid argument does not prove what we were after, namely that God is really present when lives are transformed. It only proves the very important negative, He is not really present where lives are still shabby and unchanged. Professor Hocking among others many years ago pointed out the superiority of the negative pragmatic argument.

But, if religious experience cannot be proved to be entirely reliable by the pragmatic argument, is religion alone in this respect? Far from it. I would remind you that the whole of experimental science which we revere today rests upon such argument, and faces the same predicament. Every scientific theory that is supported by experimental evidence rests upon the fallacy of affirming the consequent. The outcome is that the whole of scientific theory is probable only, not absolutely certain. But this fact has not paralyzed science, which proceeds all undisturbed by the logical defect, and, with open mind, lets down its faith upon its findings. For science rests upon faith, not upon certainty.

And this is the ground of religion. It rests upon a trust and a faith that for the religious man have become his deepest certainty, the certainty of faith, not the certainty of logic. The certainties of faith call out our whole selves in wholehearted and unreserved dedication. The certainties of logic leave our wills untouched and unenslaved. Be not disturbed by the intellectual criticism of subjectivity and of mystic experience which I have given. I am persuaded that God is greater than logic, although not contrary to logic, and our mere inability to catch Him in the little net of our human reason is no proof of His non-existence, but only of our need that our little reason shall be supplemented by His tender visitations, and that He may lead and guide us to the end of the road in ways superior to any that our intellects can plan. This is the blindness of trust, which walks with Him, unafraid, into the dark.

THE SPIRITUAL WORLD

It may seem as if I have been kicking over a great deal of religious furniture, offering criticisms not only of the traditional proofs for God's existence but also of the validity of the mystical experience of the Presence of God. But I was only doing what the great philosopher, Immanuel Kant, said he must do — destroy reason in order to make room for faith.

James Bissett Pratt, of Williams College, traces religious development through three stages. The first stage, Primitive Credulity, is found in children and in primitive peoples. The second is the stage of Doubt and Criticism, and is found in the years of adolescence and in sophisticated brain-worshippers. The third, the Stage of Faith, is reached by those who have left behind their childish belief in a Big, Kind Man in the Sky, have passed safely through the tangles of expanded intellectual vision which science, history, psychology, and philosophy give us, and have found a serene and childlike faith that stands firm in the midst of changing intellectual views. This third stage is strikingly akin to the first. It is the childlike simplicity of the truly great souls; of such, not of complicated professors, is the kingdom of heaven. It is a simplicity which is not naive, but enriched by a background of complex knowledge, not burdened or blinded by that complexity, but aware of it and sitting atop it. If it has been given to you to attain this third, mature stage of faith, you can voyage at will into arguments and discussions that are blasting at the second stage, and be untouched by them, for your life is down deep upon a Rock that is not founded upon argument and criticism and dispute. At this stage one can differ radically with another person intellectually, yet love him because he too is basically devoted to feeding upon the Bread of Life, not primarily devoted to chemical analysis of that Bread.

But turning to the whole subject, the Reality of the Spiritual World, we may ask by whom is the spiritual world peopled? Up to this time I have been speaking only of God. And, after all, only God matters. When men, the world over, reach up to that which is Highest above them, it is for God that they yearn, no matter how He may be conceived, whether He be Allah, or Brahma, or the Tao, or Ahura Mazda, or the Father in Heaven of the Christian. But men have variously peopled the spiritual world with more than God; some have added angels, whole fluttering multitudes of angels; some have added devils or The Devil, Satan; some have added the souls of the departed. Some have made two spiritual worlds, a Heaven and a Hell, with presiding divinities over each. Some have split the Christian deity into a Trinity of persons, the Father, the Son, and the Holy

Ghost. Some, like Meister Eckhart and Jacob Boehme, the greatest mystics of the West, have asserted an *Urgrund,* a Godhead, a more basic view of Reality underlying all the variety of divine forms that are conceivable.

And, again, how does the spiritual world behave toward us? Some say it is aloof, self-contained, not noticing this world, like the gods of Epicurus and Lucretius, who, being perfect — by definition — could not want anything, and would be wholly unconcerned for us, not caring for our prayers, not desiring adoration, not insulted or grieved by our sins. Others say that God and all His angels bend over us in loving solicitude, tenderly calling us back toward our true Home, that God knocks on the doors of our hearts and whispers sweet promptings toward Himself, that He assigns guardian angels to each of us, and that He came to earth and died on Calvary on our behalf.

In the midst of this welter of views about the spiritual world, how shall we find our way? They cannot all be true insights, for some of them are mutually inconsistent. What criterion can we use for rejecting some and accepting others?

Let us try one criterion — reason. Can some of these views be discarded because they are contrary to reason, and others retained because reason guarantees them? In the preceding criticism it was pointed out that reason alone, using intellectual processes, could not establish with certainty the existence of any God at all, no matter how conceived. And if reason fails even to establish the basic condition, that there is a spiritual world, it can hardly succeed in deciding the dependent question, what is in the spiritual world. Reason may establish plausibility, that is rational possibility for the existence of such a world, but reason cannot establish that it exists. Logical possibility does not establish actuality. When reason, out of her own inner resources, tries to argue for God's existence, we get such a questionable argument as Duns Scotus produced in the Middle Ages: "God's actual existence is possible. If God does not exist, His existence cannot be logically possible. But God's non-existence cannot be both possible and impossible at the same time. Therefore God exists!" I need not analyze this argument to show its falsity.

Several criteria for selecting among such conflicting views may be tried: (a) reason, (b) the judgment of those spiritually discerning souls whom we respect most, (c) the position taken by those writers of the Bible whom we appreciate most (essentially the same as the preceding test), (d) our own inner experience with God, whereby some of these views become vivid and precious for us, while others leave us cold. No one of these tests is completely adequate or sure; each needs to be supplemented by the others.

But of them all, we are members of a current which puts the greatest emphasis upon the last test, the vividness and vitality which some of these views develop in ourselves by an inner experience. This was George Fox's final discovery. All outward helps he tried, — preachers, reputedly great religious men, — until at last, when all outward helps had failed, he turned within and found an inward teacher, the inner, living Spirit of Christ, who led him into Truth. This inward Teacher of Truth is the Inner Light, the Seed of God, through whose germination within we are led into Truth.

Thus, if I experience the love of God, feeling it bathing me, brooding over me, opening up to me deep responses, and sending me out into the world of men with a new and vital love for God and man, then I can say that I know experientially that God is a loving being.

If, on the other hand, I have no experience of the Holy Trinity, if I have no direct opening whereby I know how God the Father begets the Son, and how the Holy Ghost proceeds from the Father and the Son, I let the whole Trinitarian view alone, as something not grounded in my experience.

But this test, because of its very privacy and uniqueness, would allow each individual's insights to be final, if taken alone. A religious anarchy of private opinion would result, each man being the final measurer of truth. This would be the religious analogue of the Sophists of ancient Greece, and the same sophistry is widely current today, for we find plenty of people who say, "What is true and right for me is true and right for me, and what is true and right for you is true and right for you." The public, universal character of truth would disappear. All religious groups, like the Quakers, which put the final authority not on an outer standard, like the Bible or the Church decisions, but on an inner authority, the guidance of the Inner Teacher, must face this difficulty.

But, you may reply, if God, or the heavenly order, is the originator of my inner persuasions, if all men are taught, within themselves, by the same light and source and teacher, all men ought to agree. Maybe the wide variation in sincere inner convictions indicates that there is no objective content to religion, only subjective wishes, various in various men.

I would answer in this way: All knowing arises in a relation between two things, the object out there, and the knowing subject, the knowing person here. Our knowledge of the object is conditioned, in part, by the actual nature of the object. But it is also conditioned, in part, by the expectations, the convictions, the already settled persuasions of the knower. Experience does not deliver to us a finished, unmodified account of the object. When a criminal is fleeing and in hiding, he hears a creaking

28

board as the footstep of a pursuer. When three people testify as to what they saw in an automobile accident, the mechanic will report one thing, the housewife another, and the young man in the throes of his first love yet another. And all three are honest.

When a good Catholic like Joan of Arc has a mystical opening, she reports that St. Catherine is speaking to her. But when a Mahayana Buddhist reports a heavenly visitation, he says that Kwan Yin or Manjusri has visited him. The already accepted and dominant system of ideas in the background of the mind of the experiencer is an active modifier of the report. It is well-nigh impossible to get experience in the raw. Whatever it is in the raw, it is instantly caught up into a scheme of interpretation already pervading the mind of the experiencer. I have never heard of authentic accounts of a Buddhist who had not read a word of Catholic theology being visited by St. Catherine, or of a Catholic who had never read a word about Mahayana Buddhism being visited by Manjusri. The vast cultural background in which each of us is immersed sets a broad pattern of expectation, and furnishes the material for interpretation, into the texture of which whatever we might call raw experience is instantly and unconsciously woven. And the special circles of ideas in which we move do the same thing. A Quaker immersed in Quaker literature, Quaker silence, Quaker service, will reflect these things in his reports of his inner experience. On a humbler scale, anyone who reads medical books describing the symptoms of a variety of diseases is likely to find the symptoms of bubonic plague, gout, manic-depressive insanity, and tuberculosis in himself.

Rufus Jones points out that mystical experience, indeed religious experience in general, is peculiarly open to suggestion. In this he is reiterating the same fact. Suggestion that there is something to hear if one listens for echoes and messages and intuitions arising from another world will put us into a state of expectation and of listening which I believe is greatly needed, and which is facilitated by repose, silence, and the quieting of the senses. What one hears, in this inward listening, will be clothed in the system of ideas already current in the mind.

But, you may ask, does not inner experience bring surprises, as Joan of Arc was surprised that St. Catherine should visit her, a humble peasant girl of Domremy, and lay on her the burden of freeing France and crowning the French king? Yes, I reply, there are surprises of this sort, and a certain specific crystallizing of infinite possibilities around one solution that I do not fully understand.

Take the case of Paul on the Damascus road, struck down by the vision. When he cries out, "Who are thou, Lord?" do you think that was a genuine inquiry? By no means. He evidently had been accumulating annoying misgivings about the Christians ever since he held the men's coats at the stoning of Stephen. These misgivings, these promptings had led him to feel that maybe the living God was in these Christ-followers whom he persecuted with such zealous cruelty. They had been thrust out of the focus of his conscious life, yet remained as a submerged system of possible interpretation. Finally, in pent-up pressure, comes this moment of disclosure of the ever-present, loving Deity, and the man knows who is visiting him. The question, "Who are thou, Lord?" is purely rhetorical.

It seems clear to me that some of the surprise elements in inner experience can be interpreted in terms of repressions which are released and do genuinely seem surprising to the individual who had supposed that his daily round of conscious life and beliefs was the whole of him.

But there is another kind of surprise. One may have said all one's life, *God is love.* But there is an experience of the love of God which, when it comes upon us, and enfolds us, and bathes us, and warms us, is so utterly new that we can hardly identify it with the old phrase, God is love. Can *this* be the love of God, this burning, tender, wooing, wounding pain of love that pierces the marrow of my bones and burns out old loves and ambitions? God experienced

31

is a vast surprise. God's providence experienced is a vast surprise, God's guidance experienced is a vast, soul-shaking surprise. God's peace, God's power,—the old words flame with meaning, or are discarded as trite, and one gropes for new, more glorious ways of communicating the reality. Then the subjective moulds of expectation are broken down, discarded, made utterly inadequate, as the Object, God, invades the subject, man, and opens to him new and undreamed truths. For I believe there is an extension of our knowledge of God given in inner experience which goes far beyond the limits that the subjective factors of expectation and suggestibility can account for. The new wine must be put into new wineskins, lest all be lost. We become new creatures, new in intellectual moulds, new in behavior patterns, new in friendships and conversations and tastes, as the experience of God breaks down the old, inadequate, half-hearted life-moulds of religion and of conduct.

Then we find an answering test in the group, which fortifies our inner experience. We find that some other people, perhaps the saints of the meeting whom we had scorned a little, as over-pious or over-zealous, know the same thing that has come to us. We find that some quiet, unnoticed members know this. They hadn't attracted our attention before, for we had formerly had a pattern of importance in terms of people's executive ability, or shrewdness in business, or soundness and sanity in worldly judgments. But *now* we find that we have a new alignment of recognition of important souls, and a powerful drawing toward those who have tasted and handled the Word of Life. This is the Fellowship and Communion of the Saints, the Blessed Community.

We find a group answer in the Scriptures. For now we know, from within, some of the Gospel writers, and the prophets, and the singers of songs, or Psalms. For they are now seen to be singing our song, or we can sing their song, or the same song of the Eternal Love is sung through us all, and out into the world. In mad joy we re-read the Scriptures, for they have become new. They are a social check upon our individual experience, not as a law book, but as a disclosure of kindred souls who have known a like visitation of God.

After this consideration of the checks we need in examining our inner intuitions and experiences, we come back to the question, who people the unseen world?

Let us first accept, without further discussion, God as the prime inhabitant.

I would not add a second god, the Devil, to the world of spiritual reality. I have never experienced the Devil as a spiritual being, but that doesn't decide it. Others have; Martin Luther even threw an ink-bottle at him. But I still don't believe in the Devil as a second, black god. I have even seen his hoof-mark on a stone wall in Nuremberg, in Germany, but I still don't believe in the Devil. I read in the Bible about the Devil, yet I'm unconvinced. George Fox talks freely about the Devil, but I am not impressed. I believe the Devil was devised to account for the evil and maladjustment in our world. An early effort to explain our world led men to divide the world's double aspect of good and evil into two parts, and assign each to a separate ruler. That seemed to save God from responsibility for evil, a problem that is acute if you have only one God. But I cannot think that God and the Devil could work together in such close co-operation as would be required of them if they made the world jointly, God doing the good part, the Devil doing the bad part. On God's side, God would have had to be defective if He did it in this way. He was not very powerful if He could not stop the Devil from putting his fingers into the creation process. Or He was not very good, or He would not have made so many concessions to the Devil in the process. And, on the Devil's side, the Devil would lose his real badness, and his hostility to God, if he co-operated so nicely with the Good as would be required. He ceases to be a bad devil, and becomes a benevolent, docile, co-operative spirit, really good at heart, and not too bad to have around the house. Anyway, the history of the devil idea as it appears in the

34

Bible and in the medieval Church is fairly clear. It came from Persia, from the Zoroastrian faith, and seeped across into Asia Minor, and crept into Christian tradition as an alien element from the outside, not an indigenous development.

I would not add to the unseen world an array of angels, a multitude of the heavenly host, praising God and saying, "Glory to God in the highest, and on earth peace to men who are of good will." I know that the Bible reports such a population in heaven, with occasional visits to earth on some celestial commission. But the Bible reports that demons went out of the Gadarene demoniac and entered into a drove of pigs and made them run into the lake and cause extensive property damage to the owner. Antiquated medical views of Palestine regarding the nature of insanity need not be binding upon us, any more than Egyptian modes of dream interpretation, reported in Genesis or Daniel, are binding upon us. And I find no greater necessity to accept a multitude of good spirits than of bad demons.

I know, too, that many people report *experiencing* the angels, in inner intuition and in visions. But I have always felt sure that God Himself could deal directly with my soul, without sending any intermediaries. In fact, one of my joys as a Quaker is in the removal of all the earthly apparatus of mediation between me and

God, and I should find small comfort in discovering that, on the other side of this world, the whole array of intermediaries is duplicated. No matter how benevolent such beings might be, I long for God, not for them. To my mind, angels represent the vestigial remains of polytheism, and a multitude of gods, softened by the idea of a monarchy. The time was when all the multitude of functions of God was accounted for by setting up a separate deity for each function. By and by, as the world grew older and more ripe, the unity of God's nature brought all these separate strands, formerly thought to be separate beings, into the coverage of the one Being, God. The system of angels represents an intermediate stage in this growth from true polytheism to complete monotheism. The actual luxuriant growth of angels in the medieval Church has a definite historical route of entry. They, too, came originally from Persia, from Zoroastrian dualism of God and Devil, with a lot of intermediate, competing spirits organized into two armies and competing on earth for the souls of men. A neo-Platonic writer of the Fifth Century A. D. came under this influence, wrote a book called *The Celestial Hierarchies*, which was translated into Latin about 850 by an Irish monk named John Scotus Erigena, and the whole Pandora's box of angels got root in an age that was intellectually and religiously credulous.

I have spoken of angels as vestigial remains of polytheism, when the process of movement toward monotheism was arrested at a monarchical stage. But whenever men come into a stage of belief that God is exceedingly lofty, high, transcendent, utterly removed from this low and degraded world, then they insert an array of intermediaries to bridge the gap. This was peculiarly the case in the centuries beginning with the days of Jesus. God's transcendence was emphasized, His immanence minimized. The Gnostic menace to the Early Church involved the insertion between God and man of some thirty stages or aeons, in descending degrees of glory, from God toward man. They put in the God of the Old Testament as one of these intermediaries, and Jesus as another, down near the bottom of the scale. I do not mean that everyone now who believes in angels emphasizes the transcendence of God at the expense of His immanence. But the creative epochs of angelology came in days of belief in excessive transcendence. And the whole layout of sub-angels and super-angels doing the heavenly bidding is present in our literature, furnishing a pattern of suggestion for sincere mystics. Suggestion and expectation, along with the element of surprise which I have already discussed, seem to me adequate to account for the sincere, but as I see it not reliable, reports of angel visitation.

As to the departed spirits of men, now in-

habiting the unseen world, there are two prob-
lems, first the problem of their existence, and,
second, of their efforts to take part in this
earthly life which they have left behind.

The bare existence of life after death is a
giant problem, needing a whole series of lec-
tures. I shall only say that on strict, rational
grounds, such as we used above, there is no in-
escapable, waterproof demonstration that there
is a life after death, any more than there is a
strict, watertight demonstration that God exists.
It seems to me plausible to believe there is a life
after death. For, as William James puts it,
when I reach the time for dying, I am just
beginning to learn how to live. And as Robert
Browning says in "Abt Vogler":

All we have willed or hoped or dreamed of good
  shall exist;
 Not its semblance, but itself; no beauty, nor good,
  nor power
Whose voice has gone forth, but each survives for
  the melodist
When eternity affirms the conception of an hour.
The high that proved too high, the heroic for earth
  too hard,
 The passion that left the ground to lose itself in
  the sky,
Are music sent up to God by the lover and the bard;
 Enough that he heard it once: we shall hear it
  by and by.

There would be a moral absurdity in a universe
that built up with such care beings who, through
toil and tribulation and victory, achieved a de-

gree of value and of promise, only to strike them on the head at the end of three score years and ten.

The second question, of the activity of such departed spirits and of efforts on their part to get through to us with messages, I can touch only by a personal statement of attitude. I suppose the logic of the situation makes people think it plausible. If a dear one, very much concerned with you, dies, and if he retains his personal traits after death, he would still be concerned with you, and would try to continue the life-sharing with you that he knew on earth. This provides a logical ground for expecting the dead to communicate with us. The other consideration which spiritualism offers is the report that some people actually experience visits and get messages from the dead. My own attitude is that of rejecting, lock, stock, and barrel, the whole array of experiences of seances and mediumship as evidences of the existence and activity of the dead breaking in on the world of the living. I believe that there are amazing psychological phenomena, not yet brought under the order of any known laws, which may some time be more systematically ordered and controlled, as science. But I should expect, at best, only additions to psychology to come from it, not to theology, and certainly not to religion.

But I must confess to a passionate devotion to God, as the spiritual reality *par excellence.* If He be real, and if He be concerned for me, I ask no more. I believe He cares, and that He continues our lives after death, in a fellowship of which we have a foretaste here. And I believe that the Eternal Christ, who is this same God, viewed as active and creative, is ever in the world, seeking, knocking, persuading, counseling men to return to their rightful Home.

PRAYER

We have been trying to say that the springs and sources of dynamic, creative living lie not in environmental drives and thrusts outside us but deep within us. *Within us* is a meeting place with God, who strengthens and invigorates our whole personality, and makes us new creatures, with new values and estimates of the world about us, seen through the eyes of direct and spontaneous love. A leveling of earthly eminences and of earthly obscurities takes place. The tempests and inner strains of self-seeking, self-oriented living grow still. We learn to be worked through; serenity takes the place of anxiety; fretful cares are replaced by a deep and certain assurance. Something of the cosmic patience of God Himself becomes ours, and we walk in quiet assurance and boldness; for He is with us, His rod and His staff they comfort us.

How then does one enter upon the internal life of prayer? Dynamic living is not imparted to us by one heavy visitation of God, but comes from continuous inner mental habits pursued through years. Inside of us there ought to go on a steady, daily, hourly process of relating ourselves to the Divine Goodness, of opening our lives to His warmth and love, of steadfast surrender to Him, and of sweet whisperings with Him such as we can tell no one about at all. Some of you who read this may be well advanced in this inner practice and able to go far beyond my simple and imperfect experience. Some of you may have seen it from afar; some of you may have lapsed from it after a short time, accepting the secular habits of mind of our secular age, which sees only time, but not time bathed in Eternity and regenerated by Eternity.

I do not have in mind those more formal times of private devotion when we turn our backs upon the family and shut the door of our room and read some devotional book and pause in meditation and in quiet prayer. Those times are important, and need to be cultivated. But the internal prayer life is something still more basic. It is carried on after one has left the quiet room, has opened the door and gone back into the noisy hubbub of the family group. It is carried on as one dashes for a trolley, as one lunches in a cafeteria, as one puts the children to bed. There is a way of living in prayer at the same time that one is busy with the outward affairs of daily living.

This practice of continuous prayer in the presence of God involves developing the habit of carrying on the mental life at two levels. At one level we are immersed in this world of time, of daily affairs. At the same time, but at a deeper level of our minds, we are in active relation with the Eternal Life. I do not think this is a psychological impossibility, or an abnormal thing. One sees a mild analogy in the very human experience of being in love. The newly accepted lover has an internal life of joy, of bounding heart, of outgoing aspiration toward his beloved. Yet he goes to work, earns his living, eats his meals, pays his bills. But all the time, deep within, there is a level of awareness of an object very dear to him. This awareness is private; he shows it to no one; yet it spills across and changes his outer life, colors his behavior, and gives new zest and glory to the daily round. Oh yes, we know what a mooning calf he may be at first, what a lovable fool about outward affairs. But when the lover gets things in focus again, and husband and wife settle down to the long pull of the years, the deep love-relation underlies all the raveling frictions of home life, and recreates them in the light of the deeper currents of love. The two levels are there, the surface and the deeper, in fruitful interplay, with the creative values coming from the deeper into the daily affairs of life.

So it is sometimes when one becomes a lover of God. One's first experience of the Heavenly Splendour plows through one's whole being, makes one dance and sing inwardly, enthralls one in unspeakable love. Then the world, at first, is all out of focus; we scorn it, we are abstracted, we are drunken with Eternity. We have not yet learned how to live in both worlds at once, how to integrate our life in time fruitfully with Eternity. Yet we are beings whose home is both here and Yonder, and we must learn the secret of being at home in both, all the time. A new level of our being has been opened to us, and lo, it is Immanuel, God with us. The experience of the Presence of God is not something plastered on to our nature; it is the fulfillment of ourselves. The last deeps of humanity go down into the life of God. The stabilizing of our lives, so that we live in God and in time, in fruitful interplay, is the task of maturing religious life.

How do you begin this double mental life, this life at two levels? You begin *now*, wherever you are. Listen to these words outwardly. But, within, deep within you, continue in steady prayer, offering yourself and all that you are to Him in simple, joyful, serene, unstrained dedication. Practice it steadily. Make it your conscious intention. Keep it up for days and weeks and years. You will be swept away by rapt attention to the exciting things going on around you. Then catch yourself and bring yourself back. You will forget God for whole hours. But do not waste any time in bitter regrets or self-recriminations. Just begin again. The first weeks and months of such practice are pretty patchy, badly botched. But say inwardly to yourself and to God, "This is the kind of bungling person I am when I am not wholly Thine. But take this imperfect devotion of these months and transmute it with Thy love."

Then begin again. And gradually, in months or in three or four years, the habit of heavenly orientation becomes easier, more established. The times of your wandering become shorter, less frequent. The stability of your deeper level becomes greater, God becomes a more steady background of all your reactions in the time-world. Down in this center you have a Holy Place, a Shekinah, where you and God hold sweet converse. Your outer behavior will be revised and your personal angularities will be melted down, and you will approach the outer world of men with something more like an outgoing divine love, directed toward them. You begin to love men, because you live in love toward God. Or the divine love flows out toward men through you and you become His pliant instrument of loving concern.

This life is not an introverted life. It is just the opposite of the timid, inturned, self-inspecting life. It is an extravert life. You become turned downward or upward toward God, away from yourself, in joyful self-surrender. You become turned outward toward men, in joyful love of them, with new eyes which only love can give; new eyes for suffering, new eyes for hope. Self-consciousness tends to slip away; timidities tend to disappear. You become released from false modesties, for in some degree you have become unimportant, for you have become filled with God. It is amazing how deep humility becomes balanced with boldness, and you become a released, poised, fully normal self. I like the Flemish mystic's name for it, "the established man."

But let us examine more closely this life of inner prayer.

First, there is what I can only call *the prayer of oblation*, the prayer of pouring yourself out before God. You pray inwardly, "Take all of me, take all of me." Back behind the scenes of daily occupation you offer yourself steadily to God, you pour out all your life and will and love before Him, and try to keep nothing back. Pour out your triumphs before Him. But pour out also the rags and tatters of your mistakes before Him. If you make a slip and get angry, pour out that bit of anger before Him and say, "That too is Thine." If an evil thought flashes through your mind, pour that out before Him and say, "I know that looks pretty shabby, when it is brought into the sanctuary of Thy holiness. But that's what I am, except Thou aidest me."

When you meet a friend, outwardly you chat with him about trivial things. But inwardly offer him to God. Say within yourself, "Here is my friend. Break in upon him. Melt him down. Help him to shake off the scales from his eyes and see Thee. Take him."

Shall I go on and say how far I would carry the prayer of oblation? Some cases may sound strange and silly. Do you stumble on a cinder?

Offer it to God, as a part of the world that belongs to Him. Do you pass a tree? That too is His; give it to Him as His own. Do you read the newspaper and see the vast panorama of humanity struggling in blindness, in selfish, deficient living? Offer humanity, in all its shabbiness and in all its grandeur, and hold it up into the heart of Love within you.

At first you make these prayers in words, in little sentences, and say them over and over again. "Here is my life, here is my life." In the morning you say, "This is Thy day, this is Thy Day." In the evening you say of the day, "Receive it. Accept it. It is Thine." But in the course of the months you find yourself passing beyond words, and merely living in attitudes of oblation to which the words used to give expression. A gesture of the soul toward God is a prayer; a more or less steady lifting of everything you touch, a lifting of it high before Him, to be transmuted in His love. If you grow careless in such unworded gestures and attitudes, you can always return to the practice of worded prayers of oblation, to fix your inner attention and retrain your habit of prayer. "Thou wilt keep him in perfect peace whose mind is stayed on Thee."

Then there is the prayer of inward *song*. Phrases run through the background of your mind. "Bless the Lord, O my soul, and all that is within me, bless His holy name." "My soul doth magnify the Lord, and my spirit hath rejoiced in God my Saviour." Inner exultation, inner glorification of the wonders of God fill the deeper level of mind. Sometimes this is a background of deep-running joy and peace; sometimes it is a dancing, singing torrent of happiness, which you must take measures to hide from the world lest men think you are like the apostles at Pentecost, filled with new wine. Pentecost ought to be here; it can be here, in this very place, in wartime. Christians who don't know an inner pentecostal joy are living contradictions of Christianity. Outward sobriety is dictated by a fine sense of the fittingness of things. But inward fires should burn in the God-kindled soul, fires shining outward in a radiant and released personality. Inwardly, there are hours of joy in God, and the songs of the soul are ever rising. Sometimes the singer and the song seem to be merged together as a single offering to the God of Joy. Sometimes He who puts the new song into our mouths seems merged with the song and the singer, and it is not we alone who sing, but the Eternal Lover who sings through us and out into the world where songs have died on many lips.

In such moods I find the Book of Psalms wonderfully helpful. There we come into contact with souls who have risen above debate and argument and problem-discussion, and have become singers of the Song of Eternal Love. We read the Psalms hungrily. They say in words what we try to express. Our private joy in God becomes changed into a fellowship of singing souls. The writers of the Psalms teach us new songs of the heart. They give us great phrases that go rolling through our minds all the day long. They channel our prayer of song. Religious reading ought not to be confined to heady, brainy, argumentative discussion, important as that is. Every profoundly religious soul ought to rise to the level of inward psalm-singing; he ought to read devotional literature that is psalm-like in character and spirit. The little book of prayers, *A Chain of Prayers across the Ages*, is excellent. And Thomas à Kempis' *Imitation of Christ* often gives voice to the song of the soul.

Then there is the prayer of inward *listening*. Perhaps this is not a separate type of prayer, but an element that interlaces the whole of the internal prayer-life. For prayer is a two-way process. It is not just human souls whispering to God. It passes over into communion, with God active in us, as well as we active toward God. A specific state of expectancy, of openness of soul is laid bare and receptive before the Eternal Goodness. In quietness we wait, inwardly, in unformulated expectation. Perhaps this is best done in retirement. Our church services ought to be times when bands of expectant souls gather and wait before Him. But too often, for myself, the external show of the ritual keeps my expectations chained to earth, to this room, to see what the choir will sing, to hear how the minister handles his theme. Much of Protestant worship seems to me to keep expectation at the earthly level of watchfulness for helpful external stimuli, external words, external suggestions. Perhaps because I am a Quaker I find the prayer of expectation and of listening easiest to carry on in the silence of solitary and of group meditation.

Creative, Spirit-filled lives do not arise until God is attended to, till His internal teaching, in warm immediacy, becomes a real experience. He has many things to say to us, but we cannot hear Him now, because we have not been wholly weaned away from outward helps, valuable as these often are. The living Christ teaches the listening soul, and guides him into new truth. Sad is it if our church program is so filled with noise, even beautiful sound, that it distracts us from the listening life, the expectation directed toward God. A living silence is often more creative, more recreative, than verbalized prayers, worded in gracious phrases.

We need also times of silent waiting, alone, when the busy intellect is not leaping from problem to problem, and from puzzle to puzzle. If we learn the secret of carrying a living silence in the center of our being we can listen on the run. The listening silence can become intertwined with all our inward prayers. A few moments of relaxed silence, alone, every day, are desperately important. When distracting noises come, don't fight against them, do not elbow them out, but accept them and weave them by prayer into the silence. Does the wind rattle the window? Then pray, "So let the wind of the Spirit shake the Christian church into life," and absorb it into the silent listening. Does a child cry in the street outside? Then pray, "So cries my infant soul, which does not know the breadth of Thy heart," and absorb it into the silent listening prayer.

The last reaches of religious education are not attained by carefully planned and externally applied lessons, taught to people through the outward ears. The fundamental religious education of the soul is conducted by the Holy Spirit, the living voice of God within us. He is the last and greatest teacher of the soul. All else is but pointings to the inward Teacher, the Spirit of the indwelling Christ. Until life is lived in the presence of this Teacher, we are apt to confuse knowledge of Church history and Biblical backgrounds with the true education of the soul that takes place in the listening life of prayer.

A fourth form of inner prayer is what I call the prayer of *carrying*. This I shall not try to develop now, but shall discuss later in connection with the experience of group fellowship among those who are deep in the life and love of

God. But it consists essentially in a well-nigh continuous support, in prayer, of some particular souls who are near to you in the things of the inner life.

I must, however, speak more at length of a fifth aspect of internal prayer. The Catholic books call it *infused* prayer. There come times, to some people at least, when one's prayer is given to one, as it were from beyond oneself. Most of the time we ourselves seem to pick the theme of our prayer. We seem to be the conscious initiators. We decide what prayers we shall lift before the Throne. But there come amazing times, in the practice of prayer, when our theme of prayer is laid upon us, as if initiated by God Himself. This is an astonishing experience. It is as if we were being prayed through by a living Spirit. How can it be that the indwelling Christ prompts us to breathe back to God a prayer that originates in Himself? Is there a giant circle of prayer, such that prayer may originate in God and swing down into us and back up unto Himself? I can only say that it seems to be that way. And it seems to be an instance of the giant circle in religious dedication, whereby we seek because we have already been found by Him. Our seeking is already His finding. Our return to the Father is but the completion of His going out to us.

In the experience of infused prayer there seems to be some blurring of the distinctions between the one who prays, the prayer that is prayed, and the One to whom the prayer is prayed. Do *we* pray, or does God pray through us? I know not. All I can say is, prayer is taking place, and we are graciously permitted to be within the orbit. We emerge from such experiences of infused prayer shaken and deepened and humbled before the Majesty on High. And we somehow know that we have been given some glimpse of that Life, that Center of Wonder, before Whom every knee should bow and every tongue that knows the language of its Homeland should confess the adorable mercy of God.

I have tried, in these words, to keep very close to the spirit and practice of my three dearest spiritual friends and patterns, outside of Jesus of Nazareth. They are Brother Lawrence, and St. Francis of Assisi, and John Woolman. Of these, Brother Lawrence, who lived in Lorraine three hundred years ago, is the simplest. He spent his life in the practice of the presence of God, and a priceless little book of counsels, by that name, has come down to us. John Woolman, a New Jersey Quaker of two hundred years ago, really so ordered his external life as to attend above all to the Inner Teacher and never lose touch with Him. But greatest of all is Francis of Assisi, whose direct and simple and joyous dedication of soul led him close to men and to God till he reproduced in amazing degree the life of Jesus of Nazareth. It is said of St. Francis not merely that he prayed, but that he became a prayer. Such lives must be reborn today, if the life of the Eternal Love is to break through the heavy encrustations of our conventional church life, and apostolic life and love and power be restored to the church of God. He can break through any time we are really willing.

FELLOWSHIP

When our souls are utterly swept through and overturned by God's invading love, we suddenly find ourselves in the midst of a wholly new relationship with some of our fellow-men. We find ourselves enmeshed with some people in amazing bonds of love and nearness and togetherness of soul, such as we never knew before. In glad amazement we ask ourselves: What is this startling new bondedness in love which I feel with those who are down in the same center of life? Can this amazing experience of togetherness in love be what men have called fellowship? Can this be the love which bound together the Early Church, and made their meals together into a sacrament of love? Is this internal impulse which I feel, to share life with those who are down in the same center of love, the reason that the Early Church members shared their outward goods as a symbol of the experienced internal sharing of the life and the love of Christ? Can this new bond-edness in love be the meaning of being in the Kingdom of God?

But not all our acquaintances are caught within these new and special bonds of love. A rearrangement takes place. Some people whom we had only slightly known before suddenly become electrically illuminated. Now we know them, for lo, they have been down in the center a long time, and we never knew their secret before. Now we are bound together with them in a special bond of nearness, far exceeding the nearness we feel toward many we have known for years. For we know where they live, and they know where we live, and we understand one another and are powerfully drawn to one another. We hunger for their fellowship; their lives are knitted with our life in this amazing bondedness of divine love.

Others of our acquaintance recede in importance. We may have known them for years, we may have thought we were close together. But now we know they are not down in the center in Christ, where our dearest loves and hopes of life and death are focused. And we know we can never share life at its depth until they, too, find their way down into this burning center of shared love.

Especially does a new alignment of our church relationship take place. Now we know, from within, the secret of the perseverance and fidelity of some, a secret we could not have guessed when we were *outside* them. *Now* we see, suddenly, that some of the active leaders are not so far down into the center of peace and love as we had supposed. We had always respected and admired them for their energy, but now we know they have never been brought into the depths, nor do they know the secret of being rooted and grounded with others in love. Now we suddenly see that some quiet, obscure persons, whose voices count for little in the councils of the church, are princes and saints in Israel. Why had we not noticed them before? The whole graded scale by which we had arranged the people in our church according to importance is shaken and revised. Some of the leaders are greater even than we had guessed, others are thin and anxious souls, not knowing the peace at the center. Some that stood low are really high in the new range of values.

Into this fellowship of souls at the center we simply emerge. No one is chosen to the fellowship. When we discover God we discover the fellowship. When we find ourselves in Christ we find we are also amazingly united with those others who are also in Christ. When we were outside of it we never knew that it existed, or only dimly guessed the existence of bonds of love among those who were dedicated slaves of Christ. There are many who are members of our churches who do not know what I am speaking of. But there are others of you who will say, "Surely I know exactly what you are talking about. I'm glad you've found your way in."

But, sad to say, there are many who know the word "fellowship" but think it applies only to church sociability. Such people organize church suppers and call them fellowship suppers. What a horrible prostitution of a sacred bond! Our church suppers and church programs which aim at mere sociability are not down at the bottom. You can't build a church that is Christ's church on mere sociability, important and normal as that is. Churches that are rooted and grounded in Christ are built upon this inner, amazing fellowship of souls who know a shared devotion to God.

If fellowship, in this rich, warm sense, has vanished from a church, there may be enough endowments to keep the institution going, but the life is gone. Churches can go on for years on endowment incomes and tributes levied upon personal pride. But they are only sounding brass or tinkling cymbals, if love and fellowship and group interknittedness in the joyous bonds of Christ are gone. But where this bondedness of souls in a common enslavement is present, though you meet in a barn, you have a church.

In the fellowship, barriers are surprisingly leveled. Cultural differences do not count in the love of God. Educational differences do not count, in the fellowship. The carpenter and the banker exchange experiences in their practice of communion with God, and each listens respectfully, attentively to the other. For God, in His inner working, does not respect these class lines which we so carefully erect. In real fellowship, theological differences are forgotten, and liberals and conservatives eagerly exchange experiences concerning the wonders of the life of devotion.

Among souls in the fellowship, conversation naturally gravitates to Him who is the uniting bond. Most of us are reticent about speaking our deepest thoughts, or exposing our inner tenderness to public gaze. And much of this reticence is right. But there ought to be some times when, and there ought to be some people with whom, we open up our hearts on the deep things of the spirit. Normal religious development cannot take place in a vacuum occupied solely by you and God. We need friends of the soul. Fellowship is not an accidental addition to religion. It is the matrix within which we bear one another's aspirations. Do *you* have people with whom you feel it right to open your heart? If you have not, if you are stilted and stiff and embarrassed, and have no one to whom to confess, not your sins, but your joys, you are indeed an unfortunate soul. George Fox has a counsel which I prize very much: "Know one another in that which is eternal." Churches ought to be places where men may know one another *in that which is eternal.* But in many a church the gulf between individuals on the deep things of God is an impassable gulf, and souls are starving and dying of inner loneliness. Would that we could break through our crust of stilted, conventional reserve, and make our churches centers of a living communion of the saints.

The last depths of conversation in the fellowship go beyond spoken words. People who know one another in God do not need to talk much. They know one another already. In the last depths of understanding, words cease and we sit in silence together, yet in perfect touch with one another, more bound into the common life by the silence than we ever were by words.

Some time ago I was in Germany, visiting isolated Friends throughout that country. One man I met was a factory worker. He spoke ungrammatical German. His teeth were discolored, his shoulders were stooped. He spoke the Swabian dialect. But he was a radiant soul, a quiet, reticent saint of God. He knew the inner secrets of the life that is clothed in God. We were drawn together by invisible currents. We knew each other immediately, more deeply than if we had been neighbors for twenty years. I called at his simple home near Stuttgart. He motioned me to escape from the rest of the visitors and come into the bedroom. There, leaning on the window sills, we talked together. Immediately we gravitated to the wonders of prayer

and of God's dealing with the soul. I told him
of some new insights that had recently come to
me. He listened and nodded confirmation, for
he already knew those secrets. He understood
and could tell me of things of the Spirit of
which I had only begun to guess. I feel sure
that I knew more history and mathematics and
literature and philosophy than did he. And the
social gulf in Germany between a professor and
a factory man is infinitely wide. But that afternoon I was taught by him, and nourished by
him, and we looked at each other eye to eye, and
knew a common love of Christ. Then as the afternoon shadows fell and dissolved with twilight,
our words became less frequent, until they
ceased altogether. And we mingled our lives
in the silence, for we needed no words to con-
vey our thoughts. I have only had one letter
from him in the year, but we are as near to each
other now, every day, as we were that afternoon.

And now I must speak of the internal prayer
of carrying, which I mentioned above. Within
the fellowship there is an experience of related-
ness with one another, a relation of upholding
one another by internal bonds of prayer, that I
can only call the prayer of carrying. Between
those of the fellowship there is not merely a
sense of unity when we are together physically;
with some this awareness of being bonded
through a common life continues almost as
vividly when separated as when together. This

awareness of our life as in their lives, and their lives as in our life, is a strange experience. It is as if the barriers of individuality were let down, and we shared a common life and love. A subterranean, internal relation of supporting those who are near to us in the fellowship takes place. We know that they, too, hold us up by the strength of their bondedness. Have you had the experience of being carried and upheld and supported? I do not mean the sense that God is upholding you, alone. It is the sense that some people you know are lifting you, and offering you, and upholding you in your inner life. And do you carry some small group of acquaintances toward whom you feel a peculiar nearness, people who rest upon your hearts not as obligations but as fellow-travelers? Through the day you quietly hold them high before God in inward prayer, giving them to Him, vicariously offering your life and strength to become their life and strength.

This is very different from conventional prayer lists. These are not a chance group of people. They are your special burden and your special privilege. No two people have the same group to whom they are bound in this special nearness. Each person is the center of radiating bonds of spiritual togetherness. If everyone who names the name of Jesus were faithful in this inner spiritual obligation of carrying, the intersections would form a network of bondedness whereby the members of the whole living church would be carrying one another in outgoing bonds of love and prayer and support.

At the time of the ceremony of the sacrament of Communion, this bondedness is experienced: separate selves are swept together and welded into one life. There is a way of continuing this communion through daily life. No outward bread and wine need be present, but inwardly we feed with our fellows from the Holy Grail, and meet one another in spirit. This mystical unity, this group togetherness of soul, lies at the heart of the living church.

* * *

I have tried to emphasize the Inner Teacher. In us all is a Life upspringing. It is the Holy Spirit. He speaks within. He teaches us things we can never learn in books. He makes vivid and dynamic what were formerly dead phrases. He integrates us and leads us into new truths. He lays on us new burdens. He sensitizes us in new areas, toward God and toward men.

PENDLE HILL PUBLICATIONS

Ten Cents Each

4. *The Totalitarian-Claim of the Gospels.* Dora Willson. The intensely practical aspect of the teaching of Jesus. (second printing)

11. *A Discipline for Non-Violence.* Richard B. Gregg, Manual work as pacifist training. Recommended by M. K. Gandhi in his introduction to the Indian edition.

14. *Religion and Politics.* William F. Sollmann. The duty of Christians to seek a solution for current social tensions by making democracy work.

Twenty-five Cents Each

2. *A Religious Solution to the Social Problem.* Howard H. Brinton. The remedy for social disintegration. This pamphlet, first published ten years ago, is so significant for the present time that a reprint has been issued.

17. *New Nations for Old.* Kenneth Boulding. Peace through a transformation of national ideals rather than through international organization. (second printing)

18. *Anthology with Comments.* Elizabeth (Janet Gray) Vining. A selection of religious poems accompanied by informal and illuminating observations by an experienced author. (second printing)

20. *Guide to Quaker Practice.* Howard H. Brinton. Types of procedure characteristic of the Society of Friends as a religious organization. (third printing)

21. *Reality of the Spiritual World.* Thomas R. Kelly. A devotional manual of practical mysticism. (fifth printing)

22. *Relief and Reconstruction.* Roger Wilson. The religious basis of Quaker relief work. (second printing)

24. *We Are Accountable.* Leonard Edelstein. A revelation of present conditions in state mental institutions. (second printing)

25. *Militarism for America.* Grover L. Hartman. An inclusive summary of arguments today against peace-time conscription.

26. *The Quaker Meeting.* Howard E. Collier. An answer to the question — what ought the worshiper to do in the silence of a Quaker Meeting?

28. *Barclay in Brief.* Eleanor Price Mather. (second printing)

29. *The Inward Journey of Isaac Penington.* Robert J. Leach. (second printing)

These abbreviations of famous Quaker classics contain selections presenting aspects of thought which remain important today.

31. *Quakerism and India.* Horace G. Alexander. The history of Friends' work in India, what Friends do there now and what they could do there

in the future because of the affinity between the ideals of the Society of Friends and many features of Indian life and thought.

32. *Our Hearts Are Restless*. Gilbert Kilpack. A pamphlet for devotional reading.

36. *Martha and Mary*. Josephine Benton. The meaning of work within the home and its relation to personal religious development. (second printing)

37. *Are Your Meetings held in the Life,* Margaret Cary. The part which the individual can play in the life and work of a meeting.

38. *Wide Horizon*. Anna Brinton. The relation of the individual to humanity in an age of mass-mindedness.

39. *Christianity and Civilization*. Arnold J. Toynbee. A lecture delivered by the famous author of the Study of History with an introduction especially written by him for this printing. (fourth printing)

Quaker Relief during the Siege of Boston. Henry J. Cadbury. A graphic description of a little known episode in Quaker history during the Revolutionary War.

Fifty Cents Each

33. *Quaker Anecdotes*. Collected and arranged by Irvin C. Poley and Ruth Verlenden Poley. Stories which combine humor with an illustration of Quaker testimonies.

34. *Contributions of the Quakers*. Elizabeth (Janet Gray) Vining. A simple, vivid account of the contributions of the Quakers to the United States of America.

40. *The Quaker Message*. Sidney Lucas. Selections from representative Quaker writings, individual and corporate, forming a unified portrayal of the central message of the Society of Friends and of the social corollaries of that message. (also available bound in cloth $1)

Kasturba. Sushilla Nayyar, with a foreword by M. K. Gandhi. Recollections of the wife of M. K. Gandhi by a doctor who shared her last imprisonment. (Price 50 cents)

41. *Christian Enthusiasm* by Geoffrey Nuttall, Fellow of Woodbrooke. Studies from some early Quaker letters by the lecturer in church history at New College, London. (Autumn 1948.)

42. *The Discipline of Prayer*. Frederic Tritton. An explanation and evaluation of the various forms of prayer, designed for devotional reading. Especially useful as a preparation for religious retreats. Date of publication Sept. 1948.

43. *Standards of Success*. Teresina Rowell Havens. A comparison of standards of success in various religions and cultures arranged both for general reading and for use by study classes. Publication — Sept. 1948.

44. *The Quaker Doctrine of Inward Peace*. Howard H. Brinton. The means by which members of the Society of Friends have secured peace of mind. Date of publication — June 1948.

CPSIA information can be obtained
at www.ICGtesting.com
Printed in the USA
BVHW08s0141010618
517873BV00008B/341/P